The Buildings of Worcester

1 Until recently the late fifteenth-century Greyfriars in Friar Street was thought to be the guest house of the nearby friary. Research has clearly shown that this was not the case. This is in fact a very fine example of a merchant's house dating from around 1480. It is now in the care of the National Trust

The Buildings of Worcester

RICHARD K. MORRISS

With photographs by Ken Hoverd

ALAN SUTTON PUBLISHING LIMITED

First published in the United Kingdom in 1994
Alan Sutton Publishing Limited
Phoenix Mill · Far Thrupp · Stroud · Gloucestershire

First published in the United States of America in 1994
Alan Sutton Publishing Inc · 83 Washington Street · Dover NH 03820

British Library Cataloguing in Publication Data

A catalogue record for this book is available from the British
Library.

ISBN 0-7509-0557-3

Library of Congress Cataloging in Publication Data applied for

Cover illustrations: front: *the pediment to the Guildhall*; inset:
the tower of Worcester Cathedral; back: *Greyfriars*.

Typeset in 11/14 Times.
Typesetting and origination by
Alan Sutton Publishing Limited.
Printed in Great Britain by
Ebenezer Baylis, Worcester.

Contents

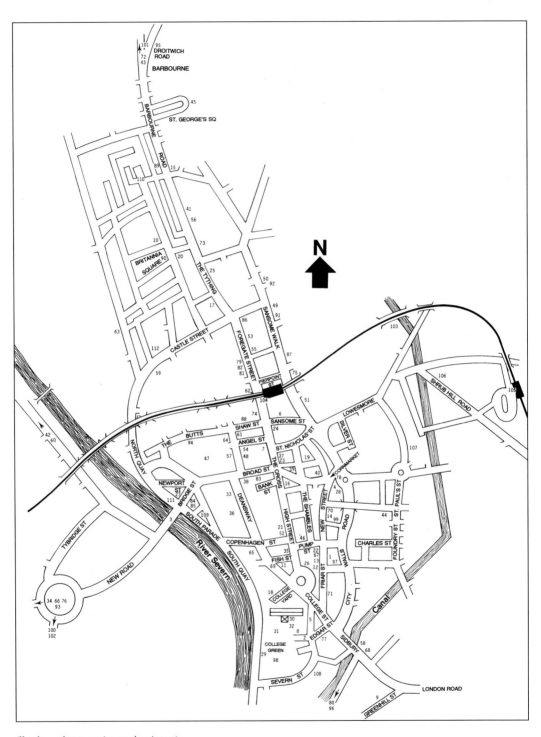

(Numbers relate to caption numbers in text)

Introduction

Worcester is a large, populous, old, tho' not a very well built
city; I say not well built because the town is close and old, the
houses standing too thick. The north part of the town is more
extended and also better built.

Daniel Defoe

The site of Worcester, the Faithful City, has been occupied since
at least the fifth century AD, making it one of the oldest
continuously inhabited settlements in Britain. On a gravel terrace
above the flood levels of the River Severn, and next to one of the
few natural crossing points on the lower reaches of the river, it
was a good place for early man. Geographically, it stands on the
broad boundary between the lowlands of Midland England and
the hillier regions of Herefordshire and Wales. The Romans took
full account of its strategic importance and probably built a fort
during campaigns in this area directed by Ostorius Scapula
around AD 50. Unfortunately, the archaeological evidence is
tantalizingly sparse, and no one even knows for certain whether
the name *Vertis*, generally given to Roman Worcester, was its real
name or not.

With the pacification of the western tribes by the second
century the fort was no longer important, but a civilian
settlement thrived. Quays were built along the banks of the
navigable river, and a stone bridge may even have been built
across it. This was very much an industrial town, and one that
seems to have specialized in the production of iron. Huge
amounts of Roman iron slag were found and resmelted in the
seventeenth century, and similar deposits are still being found
in archaeological excavations in and around the town today.
The ores were probably shipped up the river from the Forest of

Dean, and the fuel would have been locally produced charcoal. The end of Roman rule in Britain came in the early fifth century, and the rural economy of the so-called Dark Ages had little need for the industrial output of Worcester. Quite what happened to the town is uncertain, but if there was a bridge it would have continued to attract people to it and the locality seems almost certain to have retained at least some vestiges of its urban character.

There is a Welsh tradition that Worcester was the seat of a British bishopric during this period, but from the early seventh century the Britons were gradually forced further westwards. The town became the capital of the Anglo-Saxon kingdom of the *Hwicce*, later a subkingdom of powerful Mercia, and by AD 680 was the cathedral city of a new Saxon diocese. The choice of Worcester may well have been connected with an earlier, British, foundation, or possibly simply because of the good communications that the site offered. Despite these advantages, and its religious and administrative importance, Worcester still seems to have been a surprisingly small settlement – and no traces of any defences of this period have been found.

The end of the ninth century saw the early raids of the Danes, and in the 890s the ealdormen Ethelred and Æthelflæd made Worcester one of the first of a whole series of fortified regional centres, or *burhs*. These were designed to be rallying points from which to defend against, or campaign against, the invaders. The Saxon revival faltered in the early eleventh century and in 1041 Worcester suffered at the hands of the Danish King Hardcanute. In that year two of his tax collectors were murdered by an angry mob somewhere in a tower in the monastery where they had taken refuge. The furious king sent an army to attack the city, but most of the citizens fled to Bevere Island and successfully defended it. After a few days they returned home to find their city reduced to ashes.

Despite this set-back Worcester was one of the largest of Midlands towns by the time of the Norman Conquest, with a population of around two thousand people. Because of the influence of its Saxon bishop, Wulfstan, who actively cooperated with the invaders, the area accepted the new order

fairly peacefully. A castle was built to guard the river crossing – and, no doubt, to control the town as well – but there was no uprising against the Normans as there had been further north.

Caught up in the civil war between Stephen and Matilda in the middle of the twelfth century, the castle held out against Stephen's army but the city was easily taken. In 1216 castle and city fell again, this time to forces loyal to King John. A few years later, the old city ramparts were replaced by a new stone wall and the castle became effectively redundant. In 1189 the city had received its first charter – one of dozens given by Richard the Lionheart to finance his foreign adventures – but it was the construction of the walls that allowed greater control over the markets. That control was then backed by a new charter in 1227 granted by Henry III. The walls were not to be tested until the great Civil War, and the city seems to have been left more or less in peace throughout the later medieval period and allowed to get on with its day-to-day business as an important religious, marketing and manufacturing centre. It did suffer the usual problems of any medieval town and was badly

damaged by fire several times. Along with most of England, it was also devastated by the Black Death in the mid-fourteenth century.

The city's proximity to the good sheep-farming area of Wales and the Marches gave rise to the city's staple cloth-making industry. There is a reference to dyers as early as 1173, but nationally the industry was boosted by a succession of government-imposed taxes on imported woollens and expanded rapidly in the early fifteenth century. Once there were over one thousand looms at work in Worcester producing luxury woollen broadcloths, served by a complex network of spinners and carders in the outlying villages. In the late 1530s John Leland wrote that 'the wealth of the towne of Worcester standeth most by drapering, and noe towne of England at this present tyme maketh so many clothes yearly'. Towards the end of that century the trade declined, so much so that it was claimed that when Queen Elizabeth I visited she would 'fynde the wealth wasted and decayed, the bewty faded, the buyldings ruined . . . [and] allmost nothynge lefte but a ruynous citie'. No doubt there was a degree of exaggeration in these laments, but the amount of surviving timber-framed building near the centre of the town built no later than the

early sixteenth century does seem to suggest that there is some truth in the claim. That decline, seen in other towns and cities in the area, continued in the early part of the seventeenth century. In 1621 James I granted Worcester the rare privilege of being its own county – given only to a handful of other places. This does not seem to have helped the city a great deal.

The Civil War had a devastating effect on the city. Worcester's sympathies, as a manufacturing town, lay more with Parliament than with King Charles, but it was also the county town of a strongly Royalist county. Like other places it tried, and failed, to remain aloof from the conflict altogether, hurriedly repairing its decrepit city walls and hoping that the war would pass it by. In the summer of 1642 a Royalist convoy of valuable gold and silver plate travelling from Oxford to Shrewsbury entered Worcester unhindered. In September a small Parliamentary force under Colonel Fiennes made a fairly unconvincing attempt to attack the convoy but retreated from Sidbury Gate towards Powick. King Charles, meanwhile, had dispatched another escort for the convoy, under the command of Prince Rupert. On 23 September his forces and those of Colonel Fiennes met, purely by accident, close to Powick Bridge. It is uncertain which of the two small armies was more surprised, but this short and bloody battle was the first proper engagement of the war. The Royalists won the day but were unable to stay in the city. Worcester was occupied for several weeks by Parliamentary troops, and it may well have been their conduct that led to Worcester becoming a Royalist stronghold after they had left to fight at Edge Hill.

After surviving one siege in 1643 Worcester was left virtually unmolested for three years, but the price it paid was high. Unrest and poverty increased within the walls as local taxes were imposed to maintain the defences and the Royalist garrison. Industry and commerce continued to decline. By the spring of 1646, with the war coming to an end, the city was at breaking point. In May it was besieged by Parliamentary troops and it seemed certain that the end would be swift. Although most other Royalists towns had been captured, there was no possible relief in sight, and the war was clearly lost, the governor, Henry Washington, refused to capitulate. The city held out, despite constant bombardment, even after the fall of Oxford, but finally surrendered, with honour, on 23 July.

Five years later, the exiled Charles II led a Scottish army south and arrived in Worcester in August 1651; the small and totally outnumbered Parliamentary garrison had wisely left. He was not enthusiastically welcomed by a city still suffering from its earlier loyalty to the Crown, but he decided to make Worcester his base. A new defensive earthwork was hurriedly built above Sidbury to defend the southern flank of the city, christened Fort Royal. In the inevitable battle that followed, on 3 September, Cromwell's troops eventually won and thousands died in battle or were executed mercilessly afterwards. Again the innocent citizens suffered the most. In less than ten years, Worcester had been the scene of the first and virtually the last engagements of the first Civil War, and of the only major engagement of the second. Most of the buildings in the suburbs had been pulled down by the defenders to deny attackers shelter or had been destroyed by those attackers. The economy

1 A mid-nineteenth-century engraving of the courtyard of the Greyfriars, built as the town house of a wealthy merchant in about 1480. In the early years of this century it was 'in a terrible state of dilapidation', but was saved by the efforts of several individuals and now belongs to the National Trust

4 From the rear of this house on the corner of Cornmarket and New Street, Charles II is reputed to have fled the city after the defeat of his forces in 1651 at the Battle of Worcester. The building itself is both large and complex, and as well as this portion in New Street – which has two recently restored gables – there is another part visible in the corner of the Cornmarket

Ancient Lich Street was demolished in the early 1960s to make way for the Lich Gate development. One of the many architectural losses was the so-called Deanery, recorded here in the mid-nineteenth century. In the background is the tower of the cathedral

was in ruins and the people desperate; the Restoration of the monarchy in 1660 could only bring about improvements. The city got little or nothing in way of recompense from Charles II, and its motto – *Civitas in bello et pace fidelis* (The city faithful in peace or war) – was a poor reward for the hardships it had suffered.

It took some time for Worcester to recover, and this is reflected in its architecture. There are few buildings that can be confidently dated to the second half of the seventeenth century, but by the start of the eighteenth century matters had begun to improve dramatically. Quite early on in the century Defoe could report that: 'This city is very full of people, and the people generally esteem'd very rich, being full of business, occasion'd chiefly by the cloathing trade . . .' In fact the old cloth trade had continued to decline but was gradually being replaced by the glove-making industry, for which Worcester became world renowned; in the early nineteenth century there were over a hundred glove manufactories in the city. The river traffic was also increasing, and by the middle of the century Worcester's still-famous porcelain manufacture had begun. Its agricultural markets continued to be very important, particularly for hops, corn and malt. The city also became a fashionable focus for its county and had its own rustic version of the 'season', drawing in the local gentry who bought or rented the new and up-to-date houses that began to line its more fashionable districts. The population grew steadily from well under ten thousand at the start of the eighteenth century to nearly fourteen thousand by the end of it. Almost a century after Defoe, William Cobbett considered Worcester 'one of the cleanest, neatest, and handsomest towns I ever saw . . . the people are, upon the whole, the most suitably dressed and most decent looking people'.

In the first few decades of the nineteenth century the population almost doubled and continued to grow rapidly, reaching well over 33,000 by the 1860s. The city itself was also physically growing, with new developments on the outskirts eventually being incorporated in its expanding boundaries, along with older established settlements such as St John's and Barbourne. This rapid growth did cause problems; despite Cobbett's view there were many parts of the

5 College Precinct, skirting the eastern side of the cathedral complex, is a rare piece of traffic-free Georgian streetscape, and the restored cobbled surface in front of the mid-eighteenth-century houses is most welcome

6 The marketing of hops became a major industry in eighteenth-century Worcester, as recorded in this terracotta pediment decoration in Sansome Street

city that were unfit to live in, a fact brought home all too horribly in a cholera epidemic that began in 1863 and took over 250 lives. Nevertheless, improvements in road, rail and river transport, and the city's close proximity to the industrialized region around Birmingham and the Black Country, helped and sustained continued growth in its industries, particularly on the riverside and in the Lowesmore and Shrub Hill suburbs.

The twentieth century has seen huge changes in the city, not all for the better. In 1974 centuries of tradition were ended at a stroke by the faceless bureaucrats of Westminster. The ancient and logical administrative unit of Worcestershire was amalgamated with the equally ancient and logical administrative unit of Herefordshire to form the modern and illogical administrative unit of Hereford & Worcester, a huge and unwieldly county stretching from the sparsely populated uplands of the Black Mountains to the industrial wastelands of the Black Country. Officially, Worcester became joint 'capital' of the new unit but, as Hereford was the first name in the new title, Worcester was given the new seat of local government – thoughtfully banished to those outskirts farthest away from its sister city. Just twenty years later the whole scenario is about to be changed again, and perhaps Worcester will retain its status and regain its county.

Approaching the end of the twentieth century, Worcester is a thriving city in its own right, with a population of over 80,000 people. It is, as it has always been, a significant shopping and marketing centre for a large region, as well as an important industrial town. As a result it also has one of the worst traffic problems in the Midlands. Over and above everything, Worcester is, quite simply, one of the finest historic cities in the country, yet one that is often overlooked or at best treated only as a half-day stop-off on a coach tour. It is worth a far longer look than that.

7 One of the finely decorated doorways of the early eighteenth-century Berkeley Almshouses in The Foregate

8 The doorway of College House, just west of Edgar's Tower, is an early eighteenth-century example of one with a 'Gibbs's surround, with chunky blocks in the architrave of a type liked by James Gibbs

9 A plain, elegant doorcase with a lovely porch on twisted columns provides the entrance to this early nineteenth-century Regency house in Greenhill Street

10 The bizarre detailing of this house in the Britannia Square development is all too evident. It is certainly an interesting collection of motifs

Architectural Character

Its more modern buildings apart, Worcester gives the impression of being a city of spacious streets of eighteenth and early nineteenth-century brick buildings. Indeed, the long spine of the city running northwards from the cathedral – High Street, The Cross, The Foregate, The Tything and the start of Barbourne – is surely one of the most impressive Georgian streetscapes in the Midlands. As in so many historic towns, this initial impression is misleading, for behind many a brick façade lies a much older timber-framed building. In other parts of the city, historic areas of narrow streets have been cleared away this century and even the continuous width of the High Street only dates from the beginning of it. Before that it had narrowed considerably as it approached The Cross, and the east side was rebuilt on its present line to accommodate trams in 1903. There are also still one or two areas where at least some impression of a much older Worcester can be enjoyed – especially in New Street and Friar Street.

Even with all the rebuilding, one characteristic of medieval Worcester is fossilized in its present buildings. The pressure on land in the middle of a successful medieval city meant that the normal type of a house built in the country, where space was not a problem, had to be adapted. The typical urban property plot was the narrow burgage plot, running at right angles from the street frontage. This in turn led to the development of tall and narrow buildings, still the dominate characteristic of central Worcester, even though the buildings themselves may be decidedly modern.

Worcester is a city of brick and timber; it has, and had, very few stone buildings – in fact virtually none apart from those connected with Church or Crown. Only the Church and the Crown had the confidence and the finance to build in what was an expensive material. The local building stones of Worcestershire are generally varieties of new red sandstone, of varying colours though generally red and greeny-grey. These are easy stones to quarry, cut and carve, but notoriously prone to weathering. This is why Worcester Cathedral has been subjected to so much restoration; its stone has literally rotted over the centuries. Most of the building stone for the cathedral was brought from quarries to the north of the city, around Ombersley, and the stone used in the castle and the city wall probably came from the same area. Stone was also brought in from other areas in the medieval period – Cotswold oolite was used in the Norman work of the cathedral, for example, and Purbeck marble for the shafts of the thirteenth-century work east of the crossing. Later, even without significant improvements in transport, it was possible to bring in more Cotswold stone for the rebuilding of St Swithun's in the first half of the eighteenth century. By the mid-nineteenth century it was a fairly straightforward matter to import Bath stone for the new Congregationalist chapel in Angel Place.

The traditional building material in the well-wooded western Midlands was, for centuries, timber and, in particular, English oak. Over the years, timber-framed buildings evolved from fairly primitive structures to sophisticated pieces of architectural engineering. Usually, the felled trees were worked in the carpenter's yard, where the individual pieces to be used were measured, sawn and shaped. They were then made up into the various frames and slotted together on the yard floor. Generally, each individual joint was then marked by a specific number – usually a debased form of Roman numeral gouged or scratched into the face of the wood. The frame was then dismantled, loaded onto carts, and taken to the building site to be re-erected – just like a giant three-dimensional jigsaw, with the 'carpenters' marks' used as the key. These marks can often still be seen on exposed timbers if looked for carefully enough – there are, for example, some fine specimens inside The Commandery in Worcester.

11 This isolated remnant of the rows of timber-framed houses that once lined Fish Street, Tudor Cottage, probably dates to the late sixteenth century. Despite its present appearance, its gabled front was once all close-studded. Note how much more economical was the use of timber in the unseen side walls

12 The Tudor House in Friar Street has been a museum of ordinary Worcester life since the start of the 1970s. The close-studded range was probably built in the middle of the sixteenth century

13 This little pair of cottages, Nos. 4–6 Friar Street, probably dates from the first half of the sixteenth century. They have a jettied upper storey, fairly large panels, and braces

The 'panels' between the timbers obviously had to be filled in once the frames were up, generally with wattle-and-daub. This usually consisted of horizontal twigs woven around vertical split staves to form a key for a daub of clay and dung. Once dry and cracked, the panels were given a thin skim of plaster. Medieval panels were large, but the size of panels gradually decreased towards the late sixteenth century. An alternative style to the square or rectangular framing was close-studding, in which vertical posts (or 'studs') were placed close together in the frame – a deliberately expensive and ostentatious use of timber that became more popular as timber became scarcer. This type of framing was clearly favoured in Worcester from the late medieval period right up until the beginning of the seventeenth century.

One important thing to remember about timber-framed buildings is that they were not, originally, black and white. That colour scheme is largely a Victorian idea, possibly because pitch and paint had been used to protect the ageing and rotting timbers of buildings that had survived till that period, and helped to bring about the idea that the timbers were always black. In fact little is really known about how timber-frames in the Midlands were originally treated – although it is known that elsewhere they would often have been painted quite gaudily. It is generally assumed that the oak would have been allowed to 'silver' naturally as it aged, blending in with the off-white plaster of the panel infills. One interesting aside, however, is that a decree was issued before a visit of Queen Elizabeth I to Worcester that all householders should paint their homes with 'comely colours'!

Most of Worcester's timber-framed buildings are fairly humble structures, generally just two storeys high and with slightly overhanging, or 'jettied', upper floors and roofs running parallel to the street. The city has no fine and elaborately carved timber-framed mansions of the type seen in Shrewsbury, Ludlow or Chester. When those buildings were being put up, Worcester was a city in decline. Only the Greyfriars in Friar Street, The Commandery in Sidbury and Nash's House in New Street aspire to such grandeur, though the fragments of the so-called King Charles House by the Cornmarket clearly show that it once did so as well. Of

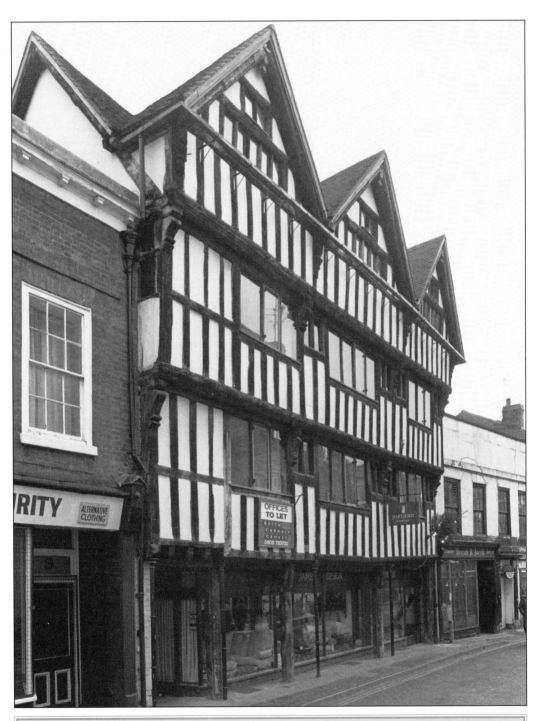

14 Nash's House in New Street is one of the most imposing timber-framed buildings in the city. Close-studded and shallow-jettied, it was built at the very start of the seventeenth century by Richard Nash and at one stage there may have been quite a few like it in Worcester. It is now in need of a sympathetic owner, and new windows more in keeping with the originals

15 On the corner of The Tything and Little London is this humble early seventeenth-century timber-framed building, showing clearly how even buildings of this status would often be given more fashionable brick fronts in the eighteenth and nineteenth centuries

course, there were probably such buildings on the main thoroughfare of High Street, The Cross and The Foregate, but most of these were replaced when the economy recovered in later years. In about 1540 John Leland said of Worcester that 'there be diverse fayre streets in the towne, well builded with tymbre'.

Tiles were being made in Worcester in the fourteenth century, and tiles are very closely linked to that other main building material – brick. Surprisingly, there seems to be very little early use of brick in the city, except in the chimney stacks of timber-framed buildings. In the late fifteenth century it was decreed that 'no chimneys of timber be suffered'. Only at the very end of the seventeenth century do important brick buildings begin to appear, notably the Berkeley Hospital on The Foregate, a long quadrangle with single-storey ranges on either side and a chapel facing the gateway. Founded in 1692 by a bequest of £2,000 in Robert Berkeley's will to house twelve men and just one woman, the buildings were probably put up shortly before 1710. The design is clearly influenced by the Netherlands.

16 Worcester had its own distinctive architectural style at the start of the eighteenth century, and this fine building, No. 2 The Cross, is typical of those of higher status. It has similarities with the Guildhall and Britannia House and dates to the early decades of the century

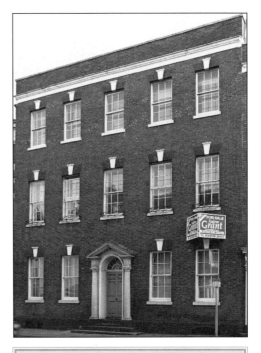

17 By the later eighteenth century, Worcester's town houses were less distinctive, though still well designed. This building in The Tything is a typical example, fairly plain yet still sporting the stone keystones used in earlier years

18 College Yard, north of the cathedral, has probably changed little since the eighteenth century, apart from suffering the invasive noise of cars racing through the city centre's inner ring road

From the start of the eighteenth century onwards, brick was the only fashionable material to build in. Those who could afford it demolished their old timber-framed structures and built anew. Others built in the more fashionable areas being developed just outside the centre of town – in Sidbury, and more importantly, along either side of The Foregate and The Tything. Those who could afford neither to rebuild nor move often added brick fronts to their timber-framed buildings; others made do with covering them with lath-and-plaster. The whole face of the city changed; symmetry and order ruled.

Georgian buildings were often based on published designs in architectural pattern books, which led to quite a degree of conformity throughout the country. There were obviously local characteristics, and in Worcester the work of a particularly skilled group of architects and builders in the first half of the eighteenth century can usually be identified by an obvious love of carved stone keystones in the middle of otherwise normal 'flat-arch' brick lintels over windows, occasionally by stone swags or shells below windows, and, where possible, stone quoins. The best known of these craftsmen was Thomas White, but although several buildings have been credited to him little is known of his work apart from his fine carvings.

As part of the general order of Georgian buildings, roof lines were, by and large, hidden behind parapets so that the buildings appeared to be flat-topped. In Worcester, the local architects clearly enjoyed using central pediments, semicircular on the Guildhall, the Bishop's Palace and Britannia House, but more typically triangular, as on the Infirmary and on several grander houses. On some of the later houses the pediments were not even at the highest point of the building and look as if they were simply attached to the front wall.

The Georgian period was a very long one, from the early eighteenth century right up until the accession of Queen Victoria. The changes in style were quite subtle and it is only really in the latter part of the nineteenth century that, church and public architecture apart, the look of houses in general began to alter. The final development of neoclassical architecture can be seen in the rendered (or stuccoed) houses built on new and spacious speculative developments on the

19 Church House in Trinity is something of an architectural aberration, with it tripartite Gothic windows. It probably dates to the middle years of the eighteenth century, when this playful style was in vogue. The modern lettering is horrible

20 In the early years of the nineteenth century stucco became fashionable and bare brick was frowned upon. Architects also became far more adventurous in the styles they used – though as this house in Britannia Square demonstrates, this did not automatically lead to aesthetically pleasing architecture. The curved gables on an otherwise fairly normal building are peculiar

outskirts in the early nineteenth century, particulary in Britannia Square to the north and Lansdowne Crescent to the east. Despite their names, these are quite informal groupings, unlike housing of similar date in spa towns like Cheltenham and Leamington Spa.

The early years of Victoria's reign coincided with a reaction against the rigidity of neoclassicism and an interest in the Romantic. Throughout the rest of her reign interest in historic architectural styles, initially mainly confined to the more important buildings, gradually spread to all forms, from libraries to quite humble houses. Worcester's suburbs provide many examples of the often bizarre results.

The twentieth century has not been kind to the ancient city of Worcester. It has to be said, quite firmly, that Worcester is still well worth visiting as an historic city not because of recent developments but in spite of them. The damage caused by the creation of College Street at the start of the nineteenth century started the rot, destroying the tranquillity of the northern part of the cathedral close. In the following decades the interest in, and appreciation of, historic architecture was growing but Worcester still managed to lose some of its most significant buildings, including the medieval Deanery and the Guesten Hall. In 1873 no less an authority that Sir George Gilbert Scott declared in a letter that 'Worcester enjoys an unenviable notoriety for the destruction of its antiquities'. There were odd successes for the preservationists, such as the saving of Queen Elizabeth's House in Trinity, but on the whole the late nineteenth century and most of the twentieth to date have seen much of historic Worcester disappear. The city seems to have virtually surrendered to the motor car, traffic is incessant, and car parks abound. It is only really on Sunday mornings that a more tranquil city emerges, and a very fine one it is too.

Architecturally, there have been few admirable additions since the Second World War to the city's building stock. Many of the new buildings are not particularly ugly; indeed, some, in other settings, would have some merit, such as the College of Technology on Deansway begun in 1959. In most cases they are simply in the wrong place. In The Foregate, for example, between the Guildhall (one of the finest examples of urban

Baroque in the country) and the busy but refined late Victorian Italianate shop now housing Waterstones, is Marmion House – a plain glass, concrete and brick shoe-box totally out of keeping with either. Worse still is the mid-1960s Edgar House, a charmless multi-storey block that completely destroys the view of the fine frontage of Shrub Hill station. There are many similar aberrations throughout the city, although except for the three stubby tower blocks in St John's, Worcester has been spared the high-rise building.

22 The Eagle Vaults on Friar Street is a wonderful mixture of early eighteenth-century architecture and late nineteenth-century tiled pub-front

23 Lloyds Bank on The Cross is a remarkably fine, and quite late, example of neoclassical architecture. It was designed by E. W. Elmslie and opened for business in 1862

24 No one can accuse the Hop Market Commercial Hotel of hiding under a bushel. Its rumbustious façades in terracotta were designed by Henry Rowe & Son and are vaguely Baroque. It was opened in 1900, a flamboyant start to the new century

These buildings are relatively minor blots on Worcester's architectural character. The Lich Gate development of the early 1960s, right by the cathedral, is a major disfiguration. The design itself, concrete and windswept, is not particularly bad for its period, admittedly not a golden age of British architecture. It is something of a curate's egg – the east side is too long and too repetitive but the north side, facing the cathedral, is quite pleasing in a way, and the tall hotel block has the decency to stay well back from the front. In urban planning terms, however, it was, and is, a disaster, standing as a savage indictment of all that was wrong with developments in historic towns in the 1960s. The whole complex is huge and heartless, and swallowed up and destroyed centuries of Worcester's heritage. The long row of Georgian and early nineteenth-century brick fronts on the east side of the High Street once continued almost as far as the cathedral close, but the southernmost ones were demolished and replaced by blandness. The medieval character of Friar Street and the start of Sidbury was destroyed by the building of what is possibly the ugliest car park in the country. Even worse, between the two, ancient Lich Street, with its timber-framed buildings and unique cathedral lich-gate, was destroyed – an act that Worcester should never forget. The claim made in the official city guide, as the complex was nearing completion, that 'The fears voiced by many, including architects of national reputation, that the development would dominate the cathedral appear now to have little substance' rings very hollow.

We talk vaguely of 'the planners' and 'they', but need to think more about who 'they' really are. Ultimately, the planners are members of elected local councils, responsible to their electorates, and that means us. Of course there are many pressures on councillors: they have to balance the perceived economic needs of their cities and cope with the demands of big and small businesses as well as those of preservationists and environmentalists. No city can stay still, most buildings cannot be sacrosanct, and each generation has to be able to contribute something of value to the architectural heritage. Surely there must be a way in which that this can be done without destroying a city's historic character, a character that, in a place like Worcester, is an important commodity in its

25 Far more restrained, yet far more advanced in style than the Hop Market Hotel is the Kay's warehouse in The Tything, begun just seven years later. It is, quite simply, a very fine building and one that could have been built only yesterday. The proportions are just right and the detailing, though simple, is executed with great skill. What happened to English architecture later this century is a mystery

26 The Lich Gate development was an urban planning disaster – even though the architects did their best. When it was begun, vast areas of medieval Worcester were bulldozed and all of Lich Street disappeared

own right – a part of the city's attraction to its tourist trade. Perhaps lessons have been learned. The latest shopping complexes to the west of the High Street have at least retained some historic buildings in their developments, and the buried heritage of the city has not been completely forgotten. The archaeological study of Worcester's past has been a role model for other historic cities, as is the simple but effective Heritage Trail in the Crowngate Centre. The city now has an active Civic Society, a good conservation team in its planning department, and its own city archaeologist; perhaps its past now has a safer future. The most remarkable thing about this fascinating city is just how many historic buildings have survived – let us hope that the new respect for its past will continue to thrive.

27 Worcester seems to have surrendered to the motor car. This is the view from the riverside, looking past Newport Street, once the principal route down to the medieval bridge. Car parks are everywhere – the street has effectively disappeared. In the background are more car parks, all part of a new shopping centre. Worcester deserves better

Defences

For a settlement that has probably been defended for two thousand years or more, visible traces of early defensive features in Worcester are scarce. Archaeologists have managed to find faint traces of Roman and Saxon ditches, but little else. In the thirteenth century the town was girdled by a stone wall, probably enclosing a slightly larger area than the Saxon defences and certainly including the suburb of Sidbury to the south. The wall was never properly maintained and at several times had to be repaired, including during the two phases of the English Civil War. Most of the surviving town gates were pulled down in the eighteenth century to improve traffic flow, and the walls between were quarried for building stone. One of the very few good things to come out of the construction of the City Walls Road in the early 1970s was the opportunity to study traces of the wall alongside the route, and to allow parts of it to remain in view and be consolidated. Not quite in the same league as that of Chester or York, this long low fragment of Worcester's wall does include the base of a small round tower and demonstrates the amount of good masons' work that went into what would have been a thing of civic pride and defensive necessity.

There are more substantial traces of the wall along the east bank of the river close to the cathedral. In this section is the Water Gate, a small opening through the walls to allow access from the monastery precincts to the riverside. The gate was apparently built in 1378 by William Poer, the cellarer, but the present structure seems to be later, possibly late fifteenth century. The slots for the portcullis that once guarded it can still be seen on either side. The superstructure is much later still. For centuries, this gateway was at the east side of a ferry

28 Little survives above ground of Worcester's city defences, even though it was certainly defended from the Saxon period onwards and may also have been fortified in the Roman era. This section of wall on the east side of the defences is by the City Walls ring road and includes the base of a round tower that once flanked St Martin's Gate

29 The Water Gate provided access through the riverside stretch of the wall into the cathedral precincts and was added in the fourteenth century. The present gateway seems a little later, possibly dating to the fifteenth century

2 Edgar's Tower was heavily restored in the nineteenth century, and this present view should be compared with the eighteenth-century engraving on an earlier page. Most of the surface masonry is Victorian, and the terracotta statuary is later still, added at the start of this century. This was not a gate through the city defences, but through the defensive wall of the cathedral precinct itself

crossing over the river, and this still operates regularly in the summer months.

South of the cathedral was the castle, started as a typical Norman 'motte-and-bailey' affair very soon after the Norman Conquest by Urse d'Abitot, the county sheriff. Its early days were stormy, though the conflicts were not those involved with the Saxons or the Welsh but resulted from the civil wars among the Normans. In 1088 it was defended for William II against the Marcher barons, in 1113 burnt down, defended by both sides in the conflict between Stephen and Matilda, and finally taken by King John from a rebel force just before his death in 1216. From then on, the castle no longer played any significant role in national affairs and was used as little more than a prison.

The rest of the fabric was quarried by the locals for building stone, and by the 1530s Leland noted that the castle was 'now clene downe'. What did remain was the huge motte, or mound, thrown up by the Normans, 'a greate thinge ovargrowne at this time with brush wood'. The castle was briefly refortified in the Civil War but played little part in it. By the late eighteenth century the prison was condemned as being too harsh even by the standards of the time, but it was not closed until 1814. Soon afterwards, the motte and earthworks were quarried for gravel and one of the city's oldest landmarks had virtually disappeared by the 1840s. Overlooking Sidbury are the remnants of Fort Royal, the earthwork fortification built by the Royalists in 1651 – now a public park and a good place from which to view the city.

Churches

Worcester's ancient cathedral still dominates the distant views from across the river – the perfect backdrop to the county cricket club's ground. From there, seen across the remnants of green meadows and mirrored in the usually tranquil waters of the Severn, it is the typical English cathedral – serene, dignified and timeless. On closer inspection, the effect is not quite as pleasing, for much of the exterior was radically restored in the nineteenth century when this great church was in acute danger of collapse. Even in the early years of the eighteenth century, Defoe had noticed that: 'The cathedral of this city is an antient, and indeed, a decay'd building; the body of the church is very mean in its aspect, nor did I see the least ornament about it.' Once inside, the disappointments of the outside can quickly be forgotten.

There was a cathedral on this site as early as AD 680, a church dedicated to St Peter. In 961, Oswald, who was later canonized, became bishop and established a Benedictine monastery. Its church, dedicated to St Mary, then became the new cathedral of the diocese, replacing St Peter's. Worcester was, until the Dissolution, both cathedral and monastery. Just before the Norman Conquest, a monk named Wulfstan became bishop. He later became the city's second saint. Unlike all other Saxon bishops, he cooperated with the Normans and was allowed to retain his see. Wulfstan was responsible for the oldest parts of the present cathedral, beginning a huge new church in the austere Norman style. The east end of the church was sufficiently complete by 1089 to be dedicated and Wulfstan then, reluctantly, demolished St Oswald's church so that the new nave and crossing could be started.

Despite the great changes and rebuilding programmes

carried out over the past millennium, significant parts of Wulfstan's monastery survive. The splendid, and almost intact, crypt below the choir, a fossilized forest of pillars and stilted arches, was part of it, and no visitor should miss spending a few quiet moments there in contemplation. The masonry carcases of both transepts of the church and much of the cloisters are essentially Norman, though remodelled. The circular Chapter House was probably started early in the twelfth century and was the first in England to be built to a central plan form, a model subsequently copied elsewhere. The undercroft of the monks' Refectory is also Norman, and retains a fine doorway leading out into the close. More intriguingly, a passage, or slype, off the east arm of the cloisters has very early Norman arcading on either side. Some of the capitals and bases seem re-used, so they may be of late Saxon date. Incidentally, this passage is now a very pleasant place for a snack or a cup of tea. The two bays of the north side of the nave are survivals of very late Norman, or 'Transitional', work; the richly decorated round-headed stilted arches have early pointed arches above them. It seems likely that the west end of the nave had to be rebuilt after a collapse in 1175.

Prosperous medieval cathedrals were nearly always being rebuilt or added to, so that workmen were almost always busy on site. Nowadays, workmen are still almost always as active, desperately trying to ensure that these architectural masterpieces have a chance of being appreciated by future generations. Worcester's cathedral actually has a fairly cohesive interior compared with most, though this too is partly due to a mid-nineteenth-century restoration. In 1224 work began on rebuilding the entire eastern end of the church, to house the tombs of the two sainted bishops, Oswald and Wulfstan, and, traditionally, between them, the tomb of the less-than-saintly King John. The style used was the first native version of the Gothic – now labelled the Early English. Here it is typified by the tall, narrow windows, pointed arches and vaults, and the thin, round columns of burnished black Purbeck marble. The quality and sheer audacity of the design is breath taking. The master mason responsible for this masterpiece was a Master Alexander, who seems to have gone on to rebuild much of Lincoln Cathedral.

Around 1316 work began on rebuilding the rest of

30 St Wulfstan's atmospheric crypt is an ideal place just to sit in silence and contemplate. It is the oldest part of the cathedral, and the most obvious survival of the early Norman church. It is almost complete, and has been well treated over the years

Wulfstan's church in a development of English Gothic, the Decorated. In charge was William of Shockerwick. The work continued for over sixty years, was possibly held up by the onslaught of the Black Death, and was never quite finished. Because of the length of time taken there were inevitable changes in design, so much so that the later elements are considered to be early examples of the last proper phase of Gothic – the Perpendicular. Indeed, the nave is seen as a fine example of the gradual transition from the one style to the other. Belonging to the later period are the tower, north porch, and the remodelling of the Chapter House and parts of the cloisters. The 196 ft high tower, once topped by a timber spire,

30 The 196 ft high tower of Worcester Cathedral is considered to be the first Perpendicular Gothic cathedral tower in the country, and was copied eighty years later at Gloucester. It was probably the work of John Clyve and dates to the 1370s

was finished by 1374 and is the earliest Perpendicular cathedral tower in England. So far ahead of its time was it that, eighty years later, it provided the model for the new tower of Gloucester Cathedral. Much of this work of the 1370s and '80s, was supervised by John Clyve, master mason. He was clearly a man skilled in marrying the old with the new, a skill best seen in the remodelling of the Norman Chapter House. The interior was little altered, apart from the new windows, but on the outside its circular shape was hidden by a new ten-sided skin of masonry.

Near to the Chapter House are the sad fragments of the once glorious Guesten Hall, possibly built as early as 1320 but probably slightly later. As its name implies, this was used by important guests of the monastery. The few fragments of its window tracery show that it was a building of exquisite quality with a large hall once open to a magnificent wind-braced roof. After the Dissolution it declined in status and by

30 The magnificent east end of Worcester Cathedral is one of the finest examples of Early English architecture in the country, even rivalling the great church at Salisbury, which was built at around the same time. The master mason was Master Alexander and the confidence of the design is breath taking. Restorations in the last century were carried out with a great deal of care in order to maintain the feel of the thirteenth-century work

30 A poignant detail of the Prince Arthur chantry in the cathedral: the arms of Prince Arthur and his bride, Catherine of Aragon, side by side

the start of the nineteenth century was derelict. George Edmund Street was commissioned to survey the fabric. He reported that less than £1,000 would be needed to restore it, but in an astonishing act of vandalism, the cathedral authorities destroyed it in 1862. Fortunately, its fine roof was to have an eventful life. It was first saved and re-used, though altered considerably, over the nave of a new church, Holy Trinity, then being built in Shrub Hill by William Hopkins. That church, in turn, became redundant and was demolished in the winter of 1969/70. The roof, however, was carefully dismantled and stored in a builder's yard in Pershore. The pieces were later taken to the Avoncroft Museum of Buildings near Bromsgrove, where they have been restored and, at last, re-erected on a new structure officially opened in 1993.

The monastery and cathedral both seem to have prospered as a place of pilgrimage for much of the medieval period, with thousands arriving to pray at the shrines of the two saints. King John's tomb, once between the two, survives, but those of the saints have long disappeared. There are many other tombs and

30 The vaulting of the central bay of the north walk of the fourteenth-century cloisters

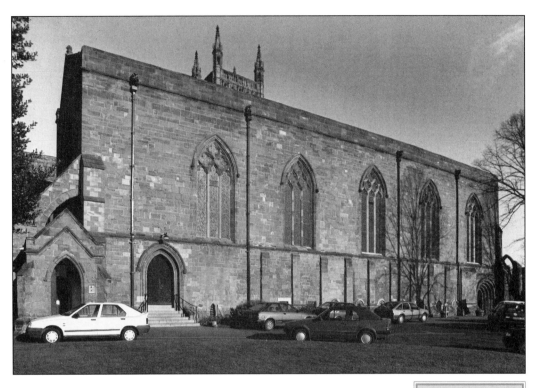

31 The Refectory is now used by the Cathedral School. The lower portions are Norman, including the fine doorway at the far right of the building. The upper portion was remodelled in the fourteenth century. This was where the monks ate their meals

monuments in the church worthy of study – none more so than the fine chantry chapel of Prince Arthur, elder brother of Henry VIII, who died at Ludlow Castle in 1502 shortly after his marriage to Catherine of Aragon. His chantry chapel at Worcester is a little like St George's Chapel, Windsor, in miniature.

If Arthur had lived there might not have been such a dramatic and drastic Reformation in England, but his larger-than-life brother Henry fell out with Rome and set about plundering the Church. The monastery was 'dissolved' in 1540, but the cathedral, suitably 'reformed', was allowed to remain. The last prior of the monastery became the first dean of the new cathedral, and the change-over seems to have been fairly straightforward. Most of the monastic properties came into the hands of the Dean and Chapter. The inside of the church was altered, with the removal of the monks' stalls, 'popish' statuary, the shrines, and the great screen. Far worse was to come during the Civil War, when Cromwell's troops were billeted in it and defaced the remaining monuments.

32 The loss of the
Guesten Hall in the
middle of the last
century was a major
architectural disaster,
deplored by many at the
time and by many more
since. It was the place
where the prior of the
monastery entertained
its more important
guests. The roof was
saved and, after a varied
career, has recently been
unveiled again at the
Avoncroft Museum

For the following two centuries, inefficient and piecemeal repairs were carried out to stop the decay of the notoriously friable new red sandstone with which the bulk of the cathedral was built. By the start of the nineteenth century the fabric was becoming decidedly unsafe, but it was not until the 1850s that a major restoration began under the direction of Abraham E. Perkins, the chapter architect. In 1858 Sir George Gilbert Scott, one of the most respected and busiest of church architects of the day, was asked to advise, and five years later began work on the fittings of the choir. Most of the restoration was completed by 1874, shortly after Perkins's death, having cost over £100,000. Although the stone used in the repair work, quarried near Ombersley, was of the same type as used in the medieval work, the overall effect, on the outside at least, is rather mechanical. However, Perkins also undid some of the less sympathetic alterations carried out in the previous century and was a far more sympathetic restorer than most of his contemporaries. In the succeeding hundred years or so, further weathering of the new work can only have helped the general appearance of this great church.

The monastery was protected by the city wall along the river to the west and by the castle to the south; on the north

33 St Alban's, tucked away off the Deansway, is one of the forgotten churches of Worcester, seldom seen by visitors. Yet it is also the oldest, and may contain fragments of Saxon masonry. Most of the fabric dates from the Norman period, and it was sympathetically restored as early as 1817

and east sides it had its own precinct wall, and one of the main entrance gateways through it survives. Edgar's Tower, at the top of Edgar Street, was clearly built for architectural effect rather than for effective defence. The name of both street and tower is fairly modern, the street formerly being called Knoll-end and the 'tower', more logically, St Mary's Gate. The association with Edgar only came about in the eighteenth century, probably because an old statue in the east face was thought to be that of King Edgar. He was the first ruler recognized as king of all England, and was on the throne when Oswald founded the monastery in the tenth century. Edgar's Tower was started in the late 1340s but its completion may have been held up by the Black Death, and licence to crenellate was only given in 1368. As late as 1393 payments were being made, apparently to John Montfort, master mason of the Earl of Warwick, and attention has been drawn to similarities between the tower and the gatehouse of Warwick Castle. The gateway was restored by Perkins in the 1860s, and again by T.G. Jackson at the turn of the century. The main wooden gate is probably the original fourteenth-century structure, although the pedestrian gate alongside is a

Victorian replica. The terracotta statues on the east face were added shortly before the First World War.

There were at least five churches in Saxon Worcester and in the medieval period there were at least four others, as well as churches and chapels attached to religious foundations. Surprisingly, in the main part of the city today there is very little medieval work to be seen. This is mainly because four of the most important parish churches were rebuilt in the prosperous eighteenth century. The oldest fabric can be found in the diminutive church of St Alban, off the Deansway, a very ancient foundation dating back at least to Saxon times, if not earlier. Alban was the first British martyr, executed by the Romans in the late third century for harbouring a fleeing Christian, and, incidentally, a far better candidate for England's patron saint than that mythical Middle Eastern warrior St George. There is some evidence that Saxon masonry survives

35 St Helen's church is also a Saxon foundation but mostly dates from the late medieval period. It was also restored twice in the nineteenth century. It is now part of the County Records Office. Most of the masonry in this view dates from the restoration carried out between 1857 and 1863 by Frederick Preedy

in the fabric of the present building, but its earliest decorative features are Norman. Although it was repaired in the mid-eighteenth century it had to be radically restored in 1817. This restoration respected the Norman features and was thus very sympathetic for the period. The church is quite small, a simple early Norman nave, with a northern aisle added in the late twelfth century. It is now a drop-in centre for those in need, a good use for such a building.

St Helen's, despite being close to the centre of the city, is also no longer in religious use but houses part of the County Records Office. This church was also a Saxon foundation, and one with a rather unusual dedication, Helen being the mother of the Emperor Constantine. The masonry may contain some Norman work, and much of the interior is of late fourteenth- or fifteenth-century date. The overall impression from the outside is Victorian, but that is not quite the case as the church was heavily restored at the beginning of the nineteenth century, the tower dating from 1817. The south and east walls were rebuilt by Frederick Preedy – probably better known for his stained glass work – between 1857 and 1863.

St Andrew's church fell victim to decades of decay and lack of interest shortly after the Second World War. It was, apart from St Helen's, the only substantial medieval church then left in the city centre. In 1946 it was suggested that most of the church be pulled down, leaving just the tower and spire standing, and the demolition was carried out in 1950. The spire was designed and built in 1751 by Nathaniel Wilkinson and its remarkably slender profile gave rise to its local name, the Glover's Needle. The fifteenth-century tower is 90 ft high, and the spire rises a further 155 ft 6 in, a total height of 245 ft 6 in. Shortly after the spire was built it was proudly written that the people of the city 'may, I believe, challenge the whole world to equal St Andrew's spire'. At least this distinctive Worcester landmark remains, looking good from afar but, on closer inspection, hemmed in by the graceless College of Technology buildings.

Across the river, St John's is the most complete of the city's medieval churches. It was the parish church of a totally separate village until the recent expansion of its larger neighbour's boundaries, and still looks like a country church. Officially known as St John-in-Bedwardine, the church contains twelfth-century work in the north arcade of the nave but most of the medieval work is of fourteenth- and fifteenth-century date, including the rather squat west tower. Restorations and additions in the nineteenth century appear quite dull in comparison to the earlier work, particularly a Mr Parson's quite boring 1841 rebuilding of the north aisle. The chancel was extended in 1884 by the equally well-named Ewan Christian. St John's was not the original parish church; to the south, at Lower Wick, are the fragmentary remains of the twelfth-century parish church of St Cuthbert's, embedded in a sixteenth-century farm building.

The success of Worcester in the middle of the eighteenth century is reflected in its eighteenth-century churches, and few towns of this size can boast four fine Georgian churches. St Nicholas's church, on The Cross, contains elements of the older church on the site, which was founded in the twelfth

36 Most of St Andrew's church off Deansway was pulled down after the Second World War, leaving only the fifteenth-century tower and the slender spire, known as the Glover's Needle, added in 1751 by Nathaniel Wilkinson. The buildings on the left are part of the College of Technology, begun in 1959

38 Above: From this angle, the true pedigree of All Saints', off Broad Street, can be appreciated. The medieval tower, and other portions of masonry were retained when the church was rebuilt in 1742 in its present Georgian style. The architect has yet to be positively identified, but it was probably Richard Squire

37 Left: The Baroque church of St Nicholas, in the heart of Worcester, was rebuilt in the early 1730s by Humphrey Hollins when this was a fashionable residential area. Sadly it has been disused for some time and is decaying rapidly. It needs a new use very soon before it is beyond repair

century. When it was rebuilt, by Humphrey Hollins between 1730 and 1735, it was one of the most architecturally up-to-date churches in the country, part of the design being based on one in James Gibbs's *Book of Architecture,* published in 1728. The design is late English Baroque, typically subdued compared with contemporary European examples, and the inside, frankly, is quite plain. This 'handsome well-built church' served the then fashionable residential quarter centred on Foregate Street. Sadly it has now come on hard times and stands disused and shamefully neglected, its stonework

39 St Swithun's is another redundant city centre church, but is fortunate enough to be looked after by the Redundant Churches Fund. The medieval church was rebuilt in 1736 by the Woodwards of Chipping Campden, using their own Cotswold stone. The tower is a pleasant example of the Gothick, while the rest is standard neoclassical Georgian

40 Anthony Keck's St Martin's, Cornmarket, is a rather plain church built of dark brick between 1768 and 1772 on the site of a Saxon church. It is still in use

literally flaking away as plans to adapt it for new uses have fallen by the wayside. It may not be the best early Georgian church in the country, but it is an important element in the streetscape and an important counterpoint to the elegant brick houses built for its former parishioners.

St Swithun's has also seen better days, despite being restored in 1959, but has a safer future than St Nicholas's. The church was probably founded in the late eleventh century and the north wall is mostly medieval, as is the core of the tower. That was refaced, in an early Gothick manner, and the south and east walls rebuilt in a more typically neoclassical way, by

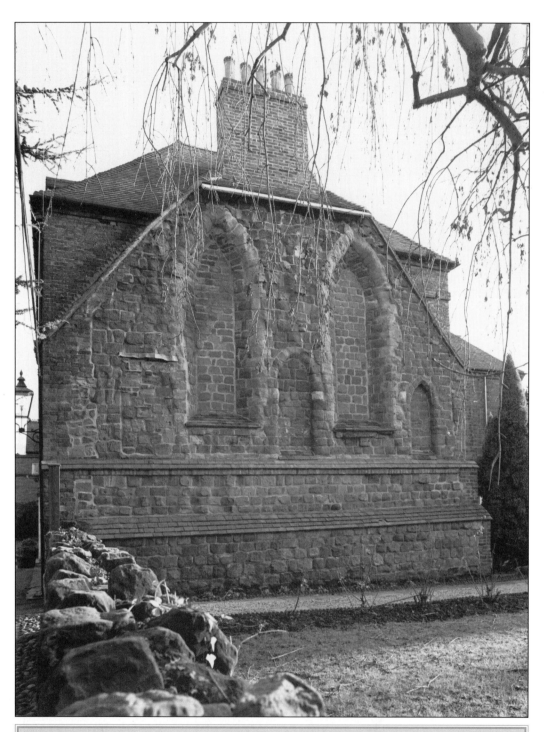

41 The surviving fragments of the Whiteladies, a nunnery founded in The Tything in the thirteenth century, are incorporated into buildings now occupied by the Royal Free Grammar School. This gable wall may have been part of the chapel

42 St Clement's, Henwick Road, is a very early example of the Norman Revival. It was opened in 1823 and the design was presumably influenced by the recent restoration work carried out on St Alban's. The original St Clement's was on the city side of the river, while most of its parishioners were on the west bank, hence the move

43 St Stephen's church in Barbourne was designed by Frederick Preedy and opened for worship in 1862. Built of red sandstone, it is unashamedly Gothic Revival and served the growing suburban parish around it

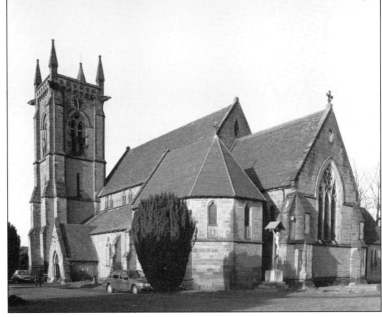

Thomas and Edward Woodward of Chipping Campden. They used their own local Cotswold stone for the work and the general effect is warm and mellow, although the design of the east end might be considered a little too crowded and fussy. The interior is simpler, a particularly pleasant, and little altered, example of a typically boxy, aisleless, early Georgian church. It was reopened in 1736. Now disused, it is looked after by the Redundant Churches Fund. St Swithun's can best be appreciated from a little way down Mealcheapen Street, which is lined by houses of a similar date and forms a pleasant period streetscape.

All Saints' church, Broad Street, on the approach to the new bridge, has been left high and dry by planners and traffic. The narrow crowded streets that once clustered around it have been swept away for the Deansway inner ring road. This church, too, contains much medieval work, visible in the lower part of the largely fifteenth-century tower and in parts of the north aisle, but it looks essentially early Georgian. It was rebuilt in 1742 but the identity of the architect is something of a mystery. It was once thought to be by Thomas White of Worcester, designer of the Guildhall, but sculptor Richard Squire has been put forward as an alternative – his epitaph records him as one of the builders of the church. Another possible candidate is Humphrey Hollins, designer of St Nicholas's, and there are certainly some similarities in detail between the two churches. Whoever was responsible produced a very fine interior in which the plain arch-vaulted nave is separated from the flat-ceiled aisles by plain Doric columns. Shortly after it was finished it was described as 'well and regularly pewed . . . [having] . . . a good light, and makes a handsome and decent appearance'. It is difficult to argue with that assessment.

Worcester's fourth Georgian church is far less grand, in no small measure because it is built in a dark dull brick made from clays from the coalfields of the extreme northern part of old Worcestershire. St Martin's, Cornmarket, was designed by Anthony Keck between 1768 and 1772 on the site of a medieval church that had probably been founded in Saxon times. That church was described, shortly before it was demolished, as 'an antique structure affording nothing more worthy of remark than its pretty set of bells'. It has to be said that its replacement, essentially a plain box with a small tower,

is even less worthy of remark. It is a shame that this is still used for religious purposes while St Nicholas's and St Swithun's stand empty.

The original medieval church of St Clement stood on the town side of the river in the Butts. Unfortunately, most of its parishioners lived on the opposite bank of the river and had a long walk to church. In the early nineteenth century this absurd situation was rectified by building the present church on the Henwick Road leading out of St John's. Architecturally it is unusual. The nineteenth century saw a revival of many styles in church architecture, but most were Gothic. There was a brief period when the neo-Norman was used, but it was never that popular. The new St Clement's, opened in 1823, is an exceptionally early example of this style, built to a design by Thomas Ingleman. No doubt the then recent restoration of St Alban's was in the minds of those involved. The chancel was added, in a sympathetic style, by Frederick Preedy in 1879.

45 Perhaps the finest nineteenth-century church in the city, Sir Aston Webb's St George's was opened in 1895 and shows an adventurous use of both material and perspective. The recessing of the main west wall of the church within the huge western arch is particularly effective. Webb had local roots in Worcester

The growth of Worcester's suburbs in the nineteenth century was, tardily, accompanied by new parish churches, the quality of which is generally higher than in most similar towns. Two of these were also designed by Frederick Preedy, both in the fashionable Gothic Revival style. St Mary Magdalene in Northfield Street, with its bold tower and spire, cost around £13,000 and opened for worship in 1877. Redundant now, it is being sympathetically converted into apartments, a use that at least retains the church as an important element of the local townscape. Further north, the earlier St Stephen's was built in a not dissimilar style but lacks the dignity of a spire; it opened in 1862.

Two later churches occupy very different locations but share a quality of design that was not simply the slavish copying of medieval work. The district east of the city wall, once known as Blockhouse Fields, was developed from the 1830s with working-class houses, and St Paul's, a typical small plain 'Commissioners' church', was built to serve it. This was replaced by the present church in 1886, designed by Arthur Edmund Street. Despite its simplicity, it shows a bold use of brick and clarity of form, enhanced by the stained-glass windows designed by C.E. Kempe. The area around it has been developed again in recent times, but the church remains.

In the much more prosperous suburb in the Tything, St George's Square was one of the best addresses in town and was served by a small Commissioners' church in 1828. This was replaced near the end of the century by a church designed by Sir Aston Webb, the man who was responsible for Birmingham's university and law courts, and, more famously, for Admiralty Arch and the present façade of Buckingham Palace in London. His new brick St George's finishes off superbly the view of the long and narrow informal square with its twin towers flanking a tall arch behind which the true face of the building is recessed. The inside is just as good. The church was officially consecrated on St George's Day 1895.

Two other large neo-Gothic churches call for little attention: St Barnabas's, on Rainbow Hill, of 1885 in brick by the little-known Ernest Day, and St Martin's, London Road, in rock-rough stone, designed by the equally obscure G.H. Fellowes Prynne, begun as late as 1909 and dedicated in 1911. Several Victorian churches have been lost, including the last St Peter's by the cathedral, built in 1838 and demolished in 1976, and Holy Trinity, Shrub Hill, built in 1865 and incorporating the roof of the Guesten Hall.

The Nonconformist tradition has always been strong in Worcester and its architectural legacy is varied and interesting. The oldest surviving building, still used for its original purpose, is the Friends' (or Quakers') Meeting House off Sansome Place. This is a typically humble single-storey brick building, erected in 1701. Equally plain, but unrecognizable for what it once was, is the first Wesleyan Methodist chapel in the city, officially opened on the 11 March 1772 in New Street. It was replaced by the first of several chapels on a site in nearby Pump Street at the end of the century and converted into two houses. The latest Methodist chapel on the Pump

47 In the later eighteenth century the Countess of Huntingdon developed her own variety, or Connexion, of Methodism. The bulk of the present building was built in 1804, in brick, but the stuccoed curved portion is part of an extension added in 1815. The building, tucked away in the Crowngate Development, is now the Huntingdon Hall

Street site is a new building incorporated into the 1960s Lich Gate Shopping Centre.

In the middle of a later shopping complex, the 1980s Crowngate, on the other side of the High Street, is another Methodist chapel – architecturally much older but no longer in religious use. In the late eighteenth century Selina, Countess of Huntingdon, developed her own brand of Methodism and many chapels were built for her followers. In Worcester a chapel was built in 1769 on Bridport. Parts of this brick structure may be incorporated into the present structure, built in 1804. In 1815 a cross-wing was added at the east end, with curved ends. The chapel could seat up to two thousand worshippers and features typical galleries supported by slender cast-iron columns. The last service was held in 1976 and the church seemed destined to go the way of so many other buildings in Worcester.

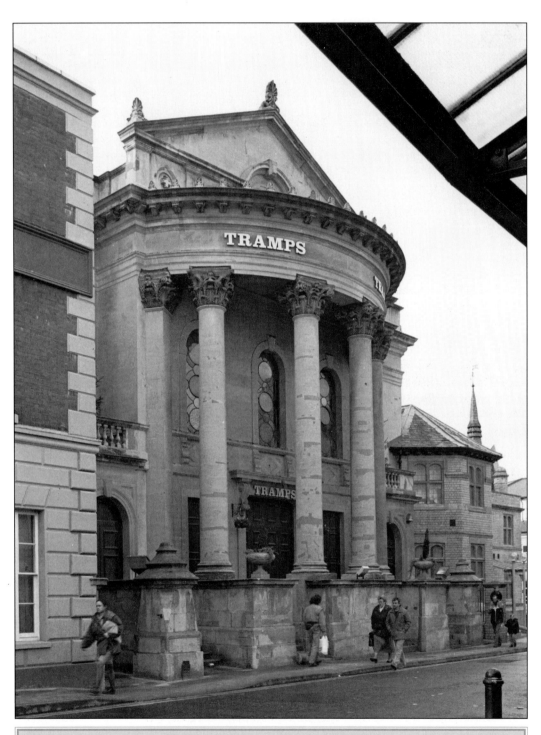

48 Splendidly grandiose, the former Congregational church in Angel Place was built as late as 1859, by which time most places of worship were being designed in the Gothic style. It could hold a thousand people but was recently declared redundant. In the mid-1980s it was converted into a night-club

49 It would be quite easy to think that this church in Sansome Walk is a Victorian suburban parish church. It is certainly Victorian, opened in 1864, but is actually the Baptist church. By this time many Nonconformists had eschewed the former humility of their architecture

Fortunately, thanks to the combined efforts of the Civic Society and the Worcester Building Preservation Trust, it was saved and new uses have been found for what is now known as Huntingdon Hall.

51 St George's Roman Catholic church in Sansome Place was rebuilt in the mid-nineteenth century by Henry Rowe, shortly after the Catholic Emancipation Act. In 1887 this grand neoclassical façade was added on to the original building possibly by S.J. Nicholl

By the nineteenth century the architectural humility that had characterized most Nonconformist groups gave way to more ambitious and pretentious styles. It would be quite easy, for example, to mistake the Baptist church on Sansome Walk for a typical urban parish church of the same date. Opened in 1864, it was designed by Pritchett & Sons of Darlington, of all places, in a debased late thirteenth-century Gothic style that has little to do with the traditions of the West Midlands at all. The tower at the south-west angle is distinctly peculiar and detracts from the rest of the building; it is not a successful design.

By far the most striking Nonconformist chapel in the city is surely the former Congregational church in Angel Place, built in just eighteen months to the designs of Paulton & Woodman at a cost of £6,000 and opened in May 1859. Very grand and vaguely Italianate, it is faced in crisp, light Bath stone and boasts a curved Corinthian portico with columns 25 ft high. Inside it was lit originally by no less than 374 gas jets by night and by a glazed 28 ft in diameter dome by day and could hold over a thousand people. It later became a United Reform church but was converted into a night-club in the 1980s.

The Catholic Emancipation Act of 1829 ended centuries of persecution of Roman Catholics – even though initially it failed to end prejudice and suspicion. There had been a small Catholic congregation in Worcester for much of the eighteenth century and in the year of the Act they rebuilt their chapel off Sansome Walk to the designs of Henry Rowe. The fine neo-classical stone façade was added in the 1880s. The style chosen for the church is unusual, given that the revival of Gothic was seen by many as echoing the revival of English Catholicism itself, continuing the pre-Reformation architectural traditions along with their religious ones.

Although Worcester, like most large towns, had many other religious foundations in the medieval period, there are virtually no traces of them above ground – although the famous Commandery could, arguably, be termed a religious foundation. Fragments do survive of the former Whiteladies or Whitstones nunnery in The Tything, gable ends of possibly thirteenth-century masonry encased in later buildings of the Royal Free Grammar School.

Public Buildings

Worcester has been a major regional capital, in one form or another, for most of its two thousand or more years. For a thousand years it was a county town, until the unwelcome interference of central government in local matters. In 1974 the city had to share that role with the equally ancient city of Hereford, in the new and unwieldly county of Hereford & Worcester. That administrative unit looks to be a short-lived one, and Worcester will no doubt soon be a proper county town again, and possibly even regaining its own county status. The city has a diverse collection of public buildings that reflect not only its administrative roles, but also those associated with commerce, education and entertainment.

In the 1760s the local historian Valentine Green wrote that the Guildhall in the High Street 'is justly esteemed the most elegant and magnificent of the kind in the kingdom', a view difficult to argue with over two hundred years later. A charter of Henry III had allowed the establishment of a guild of merchants to organize the trade of the city from their Guildhall, and although the medieval guild has long gone, the name has survived. Built in stone-decorated brick and often attributed to the designs of Thomas White (who did carve and sign the pediment), the central portion of the present building was open in 1724; the wings were finished slightly later, the north in 1725, the south in 1727. The cost of the building was nearly £4,000. The main focus of attention is the centre-piece and its amazing semi-circular pediment decorated with an elaborate display of arms.

The style, a provincial Baroque, was slightly out of date for its time. The Baroque was always far more popular on the Continent than it was in England, and far more ornate. In the political turmoil of the early eighteenth century, when the Stuart dynasty, and the Tories, finally gave way to the House of Hanover, and the Whigs, the Baroque was seen by the victors as representing all that was wrong with Europe – Catholic, absolutist and ostentatious. In consequence, the more austere Palladian style became the norm for most grand houses and public buildings. In many ways, Worcester's Guildhall is thus a triumphant affirmation of the loyalty the city always held for the Stuarts; appropriately, it is finished off with statues of the two Charles and Queen Anne. The pediment includes the arms of the incoming Hanovarians, perhaps so as not to upset the new order.

The ground floor of the central part is taken up by one magnificent room, over 110 ft long, 25 ft wide, and 21 ft high, but this is eclipsed by the even grander Assembly Room on the floor above with its splendid ceiling. The build quality may have been somewhat suspect. High winds in 1756 blew down a chimney stack when a court was sitting, and six people inside were killed. Apart from some alteration in 1791 by George Byfield, including the apsidal ends and Adam-type details of the Assembly Room, the building has been little altered. Amazingly, it almost went the same way as the Guesten Hall in the 1870s, but thanks in part to the efforts of Sir George Gilbert Scott, it was saved. Scott himself restored the building with city architect Henry Rowe between 1876 and 1880 at a cost approaching £12,000. A major part of the work involved the redecoration of the Assembly Room ceiling. The exterior of the building has recently been restored again.

The city's modern administrative buildings have little architectural merit other than their being efficient buildings for their varying purposes. In the early 1940s the bland brick neo-Queen Anne fire station and equally dull police station next to it were built on the Deansway. The new Shire Hall built to serve the combined county is, fortunately, stuck out on the eastern extremity of the city. While it may provide a good environment in which to work, its design expresses

52 Worcester's Guildhall is one of the finest in the country. Thomas White, a local man, signed the elaborate display of arms in the pediment. The central portion was opened in 1724, the two wings following in the next three years. The ground-floor room running the length of the main block is splendid; the first-floor Assembly Room is magnificent, and open for teas and light refreshments

52 A detail of Thomas White's carved pediment to the Guildhall

53 The Shire Hall in Foregate Street is presently being restored. The Greek Revival design was by the city architect, Henry Rowe, and Charles Day. It opened in 1835 and has been extended several times since

none of the civic pride for which such buildings should at least strive.

Worcester has always been a very important market centre for the region's farming community, although the hop markets for which it was once renowned are no longer as pre-eminent as they were. The sheer size of the red brick and terracotta Hop Market Hotel on The Foregate, designed by Alfred Rowe and built in 1900, and those buildings associated with it, serve as a reminder of the trade's former importance.

Corn had always been a major staple product bought and sold in Worcester, and for centuries there was an open-air market in what is still called the Cornmarket. The depression that followed the end of the Napoleonic Wars led to the passing of the Corn Laws, designed to protect the trade and keep prices high. Continuing political debate and controversy followed between those who wanted the legislation overturned – the Abolitionists – and those, mainly farmers, who wanted to keep them – the Protectionists. A legacy of these arguments is seen in Angel Street. In 1847 a new covered Cornmarket was built, largely promoted by a committee made up of Abolitionists. In

CORN EXCHANGE

1848

54 The bitter rivalry between those for and against the early nineteenth-century Corn Laws led to the ridiculous situation in Worcester of farmers and buyers having two corn markets to choose from, and neither prospered. This is the Corn Exchange in Angel Street, built by Protectionists and opened in 1848. It has recently been restored as part of a shopping centre

55 The former Victoria Institute on Foregate Street now houses the city's library and art gallery. It was designed by J.W. Simpson and Milner Allen and opened in 1896. It is no masterpiece, but useful nevertheless. The design is vaguely neo-Tudor with a hint of other styles creeping in

1848 a rival committee of Protectionists began a separate Corn Exchange in Angel Street that took just four months to build. The rather forbidding façade of this building, with its huge Tuscan columns, was designed by Henry Rowe – the man who later helped Gilbert Scott at the Guildhall. When it was finished, Worcester was thus in the rather silly position of having two rival corn markets, and neither prospered. Both were large buildings and it was difficult to find other uses for them. After serving for many years as a public hall, the first Cornmarket has now gone. In 1984 the rival Corn Exchange

56 After being housed in a building close to St Swithun's church for many years, the Royal Free Grammar School moved into new purpose-built premises in The Tything in 1868. The school has expanded considerably since, so this original range on the main road designed by Abraham Perkins is known as the Old School

was restored and converted as part of a new shopping centre; behind the frontage block, traces of a stone medieval building have been found.

Apart from administration and marketing, as a cathedral city, Worcester has a long tradition of education. Until the Dissolution, this was largely the responsibility of the monks, and reserved for a very small minority of the population. The King's School is the direct descendant of this monastic provision, being founded by Henry VIII in 1541 after he had suppressed the monastery. Its buildings are mainly scattered around College Green to the south of the cathedral, and include the former Refectory, Edgar's Tower and a selection of former canonical houses – as well as others purpose-built for the school including one range by Ewan Christian of 1888 in harsh Ruaban brick. In 1884 the school was refounded as a public school and in 1944 amalgamated with the Choir School.

Almost as old as King's School is the Royal Free Grammar School in The Tything, founded by Henry's daughter, Elizabeth I, in 1561, though the school's traditional roots are even older. In 1868 another formidable monarch, Victoria, granted it the title 'Royal', and the school moved from close by St Swithun's church to its present location, the site of the Whiteladies nunnery. Several existing Georgian buildings were taken over but the main buildings fronting The Tything, the 'Old School', were built in that year to the relatively uninspiring neo-Jacobean designs of Abraham Perkins, the restorer of the cathedral. Other buildings, of varying quality, have been added since, the best of which is Alfred Parker's Perrins Hall and Library complex, a better quality of neo-Jacobean built at the start of the First World War.

As well as providing education in medieval times, the Church was also the only provider of any form of social welfare. As early as the eleventh century, Bishop Wulfstan is credited with establishing a hospital outside the Sidbury Gate, although it may have been established shortly after his canonization in 1203. Originally dedicated to St John the Baptist, it was to provide care for the sick, relief for the needy and a refuge for travellers arriving too late at night to be admitted to the city. It became known later as St Wulfstan's Hospital and in 1294 a report said it housed twenty-two sick

57 Sir Aston Webb designed the new Sunday schools for the Congregational church in Angel Place. Begun in 1888, it cost £7,000 and had twenty-two classrooms and a large hall; it is rather a fine building, really fitting its corner site well

people. Most people now know it as The Commandery, a fine award-winning museum of the Civil War. Although used by the Royalists in the 1651 campaign, this had nothing to do with the name. It is thought that an early Master may have been a commander in the Crusades, retained the title when he came to Worcester, and was copied by his successors. The present fine timber-framed remains are of varying dates, but the best are undoubtedly part of a major reconstruction in the late fifteenth century.

The magnificent Great Hall was the focal point of the later hospital. It has five bays, a dais at one end and a fine hammer-beam roof. The roof had to be altered in the last century, with

58 The Great Hall of The Commandery was the result of a major refurbishment of the hospital at the end of the fifteenth century. Heated by a fire in an open hearth, it has a fine hammer-beam roof. However, in the nineteenth century it was felt that the roof needed strengthening, so the ends of the 'hammers' were joined by a new tie-beam, giving the roof its hybrid appearance

58 In any medieval hall there was a hierarchy, with a high and low end. This fine bay window lit the high end of the hall

beams inserted between the ends of the hammer-beams to
create tie-beams; despite the care with which this was done, the
junctions are still clear. The 'high' end of the hall was lit by
two huge oriels on each side, one of which survives, and there
were also smaller windows. Heat came from a central hearth,
and in the roof is the evidence for two smoke louvres. The
first-floor solar is of similar quality and was part of the private
quarters of the master. One other unusual room on the upper
floor is the 'painted chamber', with rich – if naive – paintings
of religious figures on the plaster of walls and ceiling. Many
other rooms in the building are now redecorated as displays,
using material found on the site, such as two fine staircases and
much seventeenth-century panelling.

Not long after the rebuilding of St Wulfstan's Hospital, the
foundation was closed by Henry VIII and sold. It came into the
hands of the Wylde family who owned it for over two
centuries, creating a large house out of the complex. Later,

60 Forbidding and austere, the Royal Albert Orphanage in the Henwick Road was home to seventy-six unfortunate children. The Gothic design, worthy of any late-night horror movie, was the work of William Watkin. It opened its doors in 1869 but is now a youth hostel, so somewhat cheerier

61 The Scala Theatre on the corner of Angel Place and Shaw Street was a cinema, opened in 1922 and closed just over half a century later. It has fortunately found other uses. The style has a hint of the French in it

parts were used for industrial purposes, and a driveway was even inserted through the Great Hall itself. Some restoration work took place in the 1930s and 1950s, and in 1973 it was bought by the city which completely renovated the structure. It reopened as The Commandery Museum in 1977. It stands as a remarkably intact, and very rare, example of a late medieval hospital; the only major missing ingredient is the church of St Catherine that once belonged to it.

Another medieval hospital, originally for lepers, also survived the Dissolution but managed to remain a charitable institution, effectively providing long-term accommodation for

the aged and infirm. Founded in the mid-thirteenth century and dedicated first to St Mary and then to St Oswald, the hospital, sited in The Tything, was rebuilt just before the Civil War. Damaged during the hostilities, these buildings survived until the present quadrangle was put up in 1873–4 to the designs of Henry Rowe (the younger).

After the Dissolution, care for the sick and elderly was no longer in the hands of the Church and the unfortunate had to rely on secular charities. Several medieval hospitals, such as St Oswald's, had eventually catered for the elderly and in the sixteenth and seventeenth centuries several other bequests led to the setting up of more places for them. Worcester has several almshouses of varying dates and styles, the most modern of which are the rebuilt New Street Hospital, refounded by John Nash in 1661. The present run of plain brick dwellings was built about thirty years ago.

In 1746 Worcester became one of the first towns in the

country to have its own public infirmary, paid for by fund-
raising and located in premises in Silver Street, now just off
the City Walls Road. Parts survive, but 250 years of alternative
uses have left little trace of the original layout. The site proved
too cramped as the number of patients increased and a new site
was acquired off what is now Castle Street. Local architect
Anthony Keck was appointed to design the new hospital, built
at a cost of £6,085 9s 9d and opened in 1770. Thomas Nash,
the county historian, said shortly afterwards that 'The
Infirmary holds a very respectable rank among the ornamental
structures of the City'. Nowadays, it is difficult to see this from
most angles, as later alterations have blocked in the view of the
original block on three sides, and only two-thirds of the other
entrance façade can be seen clearly. Despite this, it is
gratifying to see the building still used for its original purpose,
and, indeed, to see a hospital still in the heart of the city, where
it belongs, and not relegated to the outskirts.

64 The best-used of all public buildings are undoubtedly the public conveniences. This little range in Angel Place is a rather nice example. Built shortly after this area was replanned in 1913, there is a hint of the Baroque in the terracotta decoration. Inside, the facilities are well up to modern standards

Public buildings are not just confined to the serious issues of life, and Worcester has no less than five cinemas built in the first half of this century, though three have found alternative uses in the past thirty years or so. The ones in the suburbs of Northwick and St John's are fairly humble affairs, but two of those in the city centre aspired to some grandeur. The former Scala Theatre, on the corner of Shaw Street and Angel Place, was a cinema and opened – for silent films, obviously – in 1922. It was in use for just over half a century before being closed in 1973 and adapted for new uses. The Odeon, on The Foregate, is a fine example of that company's bold brick house style. Work started in March 1939, but stopped during the war when the unfinished carcase was used for storage. The cinema finally opened soon after the war ended, and it is so good to see a cinema still being used for what it was designed for, and not converted to the dreaded bingo!

Houses

Worcester's commercial success in the sixteenth century is one reason why it has very few surviving medieval houses. The wealthier owners simply rebuilt in the latest style of the day, just as, in the recovery of the early eighteenth century, their decendants rebuilt their old timber-framed houses in brick. Nevertheless, in the former Bishop's Palace, just to the north of the cathedral, the city has, unexpectedly, the remains of what was an extremely fine medieval house. Unexpectedly, because there is no hint of its real age in the stone-built early eighteenth-century frontage block that faces Deansway.

Tradition has it that the Saxon bishops of Worcester lived in a palace on this site, but the oldest portions of the standing structure probably date back to the late thirteenth century. In 1271 the then bishop, Godfrey Giffard, obtained a licence from a very elderly Henry III to crenellate (that is, to fortify) his palace, and all evidence points to this being connected with its reconstruction. The best surviving features are the stone-vaulted undercrofts below the hall and adjacent ranges, the great hall with its fine roof having been restored and altered on several occasions. Other remains of this period include the chancel of the private chapel. This was clearly a very large building – literally a palace – and it is difficult to work out exactly what each section was used for and which parts date to which period. The frontage block was added in the time of Bishop John Hough and started shortly after he became bishop in 1717. The eleven bay stone façade with its odd segmental pediment over the centre has been attributed to the same architect of the Guildhall or Britannia House, but lacks their quality of design. Recent research shows that it was built by William Smith of Warwick; he usually built to other people's

65 The façade of the Bishop's Palace was probably designed by the Warwick architect and mason William Smith and was finished some time after 1717. The design is rather clumsy, and not helped by the huge semi-circular pediment. The palace became the Deanery in 1846

65 The rear elevation of the Bishop's Palace helps to show its true age. Behind the early eighteenth-century façade are the substantial remains of a late thirteenth-century mansion

66 Nos. 43–9 St John's has recently been restored and is one of the oldest houses in the city, probably dating back to the fifteenth century. To the right of the doorway was the hall, originally open to the roof. To the left was a two storey bay, with a chamber on the first floor above a shop and the cross-passage. The 'high' end was probably to the right of the hall

designs, such as those of his more famous brother, Francis, but the slightly ungainly design may indicate that in this case he was also responsible for the architecture. In 1842, following the report of a Royal Commission, the Bishop of Worcester, then Henry Pepys, was told to choose between his two palaces. He chose to keep Hartlebury Castle, a few miles to the north of the city. The old palace became the Deanery in 1846, leading indirectly to the demolition of the ancient Deanery in the College Green and the adjacent Guesten Hall.

Unlike the obvious complexity of a medieval Bishop's Palace, most medieval town houses of the reasonably well-to-do had a relatively simple plan. Everything revolved around the communal hall, usually a lofty single-storey room heated by an open fire in the middle whose smoke eventually found its way outside through a louvre in the top of the open roof. In this hall meals were eaten, guests were entertained and lives were

67 This timber-framed range on Friar Street probably dates to the late fifteenth century, and has typically large medieval panels and quite wide jetties. The middle portion is probably a hall, with a cross-wing, No. 32, at the far end. A small section of wattle-and-daub has been left exposed in the gabled range on the left

lived. The owner usually sat at one end, the 'high' end, of the hall. At the opposite, or 'low', end, there was a cross-passage, with the main front door at one end and a back door at the other. The grandeur that some halls aspired to can still be appreciated in the Great Hall of The Commandery, built quite late in the fifteenth century. At either end of the hall were flanking wings, usually of two storeys. Beyond the cross-passage was the service wing, usually with a large chamber on the first floor above two store rooms – the buttery and pantry. Behind the 'high' end of the hall the other wing contained the private quarters of the owner and is generally called the 'solar', although the word simply meant an upper room. The first-floor solar of The Commandery is of exceptionally high status.

68 Purporting to date from 1420, this twin-gabled building in Sidbury is probably of much later date. The gables probably date to the early seventeenth century or only a little before

69 The Farrier's Arms in Fish Street probably dates to the early seventeenth century but has clearly been repaired many times. It is a shame that the rest of the street has been allowed to become rather barren, with too many gaps

70 The Pheasant in New Street looks to date from the last quarter of the sixteenth century and is a good example of close-studded framing and shallow jetties. The weatherboarding on the exposed gable end is quite attractive as well

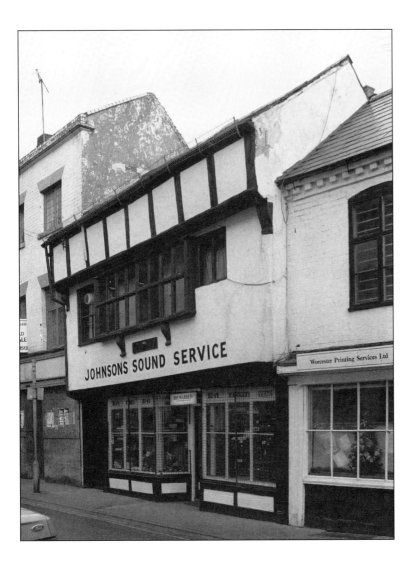

71 Once in Sidbury but now, after the redevelopments of the 1960s, in Friar Street, this late timber-framed building bears the date 1642. To build at this time must have required a great deal of confidence – and the house survived the troubles of the Civil War period

In the confined property boundaries of the town, this general pattern had to be adapted to suit the restrictions. It is a little ironic, therefore, that the few surviving examples in the city were built in the suburbs where this pressure was not felt, and could be built along the street. The best example, naturally timber-framed, is in St John's, and has recently been restored. Nos. 43–9 St John's are all part of one fairly small medieval house of unknown date, but possibly fifteenth century. It consisted of an open hall in the middle, with, at one end, a first-floor chamber over possibly a shop and the cross-passage.

7 Berkeley's Almshouses in The Foregate were funded in 1692 but the buildings were not finished until around 1710. The benefactor was Robert Berkeley of Spetchley. The small single-storey houses were for twelve men, and just one woman. At the west end is the chapel, opposite the eastern gateway on The Foregate itself. Berkeley spent some time in the Netherlands, though whether he influenced the vaguely Flemish design is unknown, though unlikely

72 Paradise Row in Barbourne is perhaps the best early eighteenth-century terrace in the city. It is actually longer than it looks; the pub on the south end (just visible to the right) is only encased in mock timber-framing of twentieth-century date

73 Britannia House in The Tything is now part of the Alice Ottley School but when it was built in the early eighteenth century would have been one of the finest houses in Worcester. Thomas White carved the Britannia that gave the house its name. The delicate shells beneath the windows, the straight stone quoins, and the stone keystones are all elements that continued to be used in Worcester's architecture throughout the Georgian period

The chamber has a very fine wall-painting, almost Chinese in character, of what seems to be a stork; a rabbit or hare also appears in the picture, which is presumably an allegory. At the opposite end of the hall was another 'wing', possibly the solar, but this was probably rebuilt when the whole house was modernized in the late sixteenth century. During this period a first floor was inserted into the hall and the open hearth replaced by a rather fine stone chimney-piece decorated with heraldic painting. The building was restored at the end of the 1970s and now houses Age Concern's charity shop; it is also a delightful place to stop off for a cup of tea.

Also in St John's is a surviving cross-wing of another medieval house, No. 6. Probably of early sixteenth-century date, its façade has been heavily restored. The hall and solar to which it belonged are now covered by a modern supermarket; the solar, at least, was considerably older, having a crown-post roof typical, in this region, of the fourteenth century. This roof, at least, has been saved and now belongs to the Avoncroft Museum.

The basic layout of hall and cross-wings evolved in several different ways, but gradually the communal medieval life went out of favour as privacy became more and more important. The

old open halls were floored in to create more space, and provided warmer and less smoky accommodation with the widespread acceptance of the enclosed chimney. Separate rooms designed for specific purposes became normal. The hall was replaced by a parlour, or withdrawing room – or both, though this was often still referred to as the hall for a time. Meals were taken in the dining-room, and cooked in a kitchen that was part of the main house and no longer a separate structure as it had been previously. The buttery and pantry remained, and on the upper floors were the bedchambers and closets. These developments were clearly well under way when the best and most complete medieval house in the centre of the city was built.

The Greyfriars, on Friar Street, is not, as has until recently been claimed, the guest house of the Greyfriars (or Franciscan)

74 No. 39 The Foregate is one of the best early Georgian houses in Worcester, though perhaps not the grandest. The windows of the first floor are the tallest in the building, following the fashion in many houses of making the first floor the grandest – the *piano nobile*. The balcony, with its 'hearts and honeysuckle' pattern, is a later addition of the early nineteenth century

75 Sansome House on Sansome Walk is now divided into two. Built in the mid-eighteenth century it was originally just outside the centre of the city. Now it is hemmed in by the railway line, just out of picture to the right, and its former gardens have been built over

76 Opposite the church in St John's is this rather fine early Georgian house of five bays. Two storeys high, it also has dormers lighting the attic rooms and, miraculously, has kept its iron railings. The sashes in the windows may be replacements for the original ones, being rather thin for the date of the house

77 No. 3 Edgar Street is dated 1732 on the keystone above the central first-floor window. In most respects it is a standard high-status Georgian town house, but the large ground-floor windows are slightly unusual as they do not fit in with the overall symmetry of the design

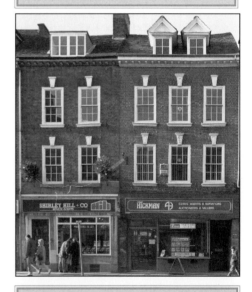

78 On the eastern boundary of the Cornmarket, this once magnificent early Georgian house has seen better days. The straight quoins, decorated shells beneath the windows and the keystones over them are reminiscent of Britannia House, and could perhaps have been by the same architect

79 No. 45 Foregate Street is not particularly special, just a fairly standard early Georgian three bay town house, next to a two bay example of similar vintage. What makes these buildings special is that they are part of a very fine streetscape stretching from the cathedral close, through the heart of Worcester, and well out into what was then the countryside

80 Haresfield House in Bath Road is dated 1740 above the doorcase, built when this was being developed as a fashionable residential area. Unusually, the window lintels are segmental rather than flat, as is more often the case in Worcester

81 No. 37 Foregate Street has a rather odd pediment, sited below the parapet and looking as if it is stuck onto the brickwork. The building dates to the mid-Georgian period, and the loss of the original glazing bars is to be very much regretted. The resulting blind plate glass is most off-putting

82 The large five bay pedimented front of No. 43 Foregate Street dates from the middle of the eighteenth century. It was later the home of Sir Charles Harting, founder of the British Medical Association

83 Four storeys high, topped by a belvedere, and just one bay wide, No. 61 Broad Street is unique. Built sometime in the middle of the eighteenth century it has peculiar Venetian windows with Gothic glazing, each topped by a life-like carving of a head

84 When the new bridge was built towards the end of the eighteenth century by John Gwynne, that architect also designed the new approach road, Bridge Street. This was flanked by long terraces of three storey houses with attics. This is the terrace on the south side of the road

friary that once stood nearby, but the house of a wealthy merchant built in around 1480. It is without doubt the best timber-framed building in Worcester, and one of the finest in the region. Much has been restored because in the late nineteenth century it was subdivided into small shops and had become little more than a slum. In the middle of this century it was saved by being bought by W. Thompson, and presented to the Worcestershire Archaeological Society; further restoration was carried out by another member of the society, Matley Moore, and the house was eventually given to the National Trust. Its close-studded street frontage is nearly 70 ft long, with a continuous, coved, jetty carrying the first floor and flanking gables at either end. A long twelve-light window lights the middle chamber of the first floor. A passageway pierces the building to provide access to warehouses at the rear, and in the brackets flanking this archway are the carved initials of Thomas Green, the rich brewer whose home it originally was, and his wife, Elizabeth.

In contrast to the grandeur of the Greyfriars, most of the surviving houses of the same period, and a little later, are

85 The rear elevations of the Bridge Street terrace are very different than the front ones. The changes in window height are due to the site of the various staircases

86 This house on The Foregate, facing Castle Street, was originally a large seven bay building centred on the central three bay pediment. It was built in the mid-eighteenth century and later extended for two bays to the right

87 Even though this
short terrace in Sansome
Walk was probably built
very late in the Georgian
period, it three houses
still retain the typical
Worcester stone
keystones. The ground
floor is 'rusticated' –
stuccoed and lined to
resemble stone

smaller and less ambitious, though it is always important to
realize that their owners would, nevertheless, be families of
some stature in the community.

The general layout of houses changed remarkably little after
the sixteenth century. A handful of large late sixteenth- and
early seventeenth-century houses have survived, especially on
Friar Street and New Street, including the once magnificent
King Charles House. This was badly damaged by fire in 1799,
and now it is difficult to realize that the small fragment in the
corner of the Cornmarket and the double-gabled façade a little
way up New Street are all part of the same house. It was, like
the Greyfriars, built by a wealthy brewer, in this case Richard
Durrant, and originally had two storeys. It was extended and
possibly divided into two shortly before the Civil War, and an

88 In Shaw Street are two sets of early nineteenth-century semi-detached houses, dignified by a Greek Revival porch made to look like a single entrance but actually containing the doors to both houses. The architect may have been Richard Morton

89 Old Baskerville, a mid- to late eighteenth-century five bay detached house, looks as if it could be the manor-house or rectory of a small village, but it was built just off Barbourne to the north of the city centre

90 The architecture of the Britannia Square development of the early nineteenth century can be politely described as eccentric. This house, for example, has vaguely Egyptian motifs with a touch of the Greek Revival

additional attic-gabled storey added. Its present name stems from the tradition that it was used by Charles II in 1651, and that from it he escaped the victorious Roundheads as the city fell. Nash's House, an early seventeenth-century house further south in New Street, is historically less interesting but architecturally more complete. Right at the end of Friar Street, in a part formerly in Sidbury, is a timber-framed house dated 1642, an unusually turbulent year in which to lay out money on a house.

The tardy arrival of brick as a fashionable building material altered the face of Worcester, but not the basic internal layout of its houses. One noticeable change was the construction of terraces of houses, such as the early eighteenth-century Paradise Row in Barbourne. However, the terrace was never

92 Northfield Street was laid out in the later nineteenth century after the demise of the Arboretum venture

93 Pitmaston House was built in the early nineteenth century for an eccentric horticulturist, John Williams, commemorated still for his 'William' pears. The house is a mix of Georgian and neo-Tudor with some rather bizarre flourishes. The once fine gardens are no more, just playing fields. The house is now a teachers' centre

94 On the ridge that once carried the north section of the city wall, overlooking the Butts, this busy mid-Victorian front was added to an earlier Georgian building. North Wall House was later a school but now looks in need of some urgent repairs

95 Middle-class housing in the suburbs often resorted to grandiose designs, such as this one of 1892 on the Droitwich Road just north of Barbourne

96 The gatehouse to Battenhall Lodge is a wonderfully lively, if a little silly, piece of late nineteenth-century architectural bravado. It combines many different materials and even more styles, but is certainly not boring

97 Laslett's Almshouses off Union Street have had an eventful past. They originally occupied the former semi-circular gaol from the 1860s, but in 1911 this new courtyard complex was built on the site. The pleasant mock-Tudor cottages are centred on the chapel

98 Castle House, on the south side of the Close, has more than a hint of the Arts and Crafts movement and was built early in this century to the designs of Alfred Hill Parker

99 The new Nash's Almshouses off New Street were built in the 1960s, and while they may provide far better accommodation for their inhabitants, they lack any architectural flair

particularly popular in the city as it was elsewhere. The individual house, whether built in its own grounds in the outskirts or in the confined space of the old burgage plots in the centre, continued to be popular. On the outskirts many houses could have been built in the middle of the countryside and only recently have their once spacious grounds been impinged on. Perhaps the best of these is Britannia House in The Tything, attributed to Thomas White, and now part of the Alice Ottley School for Girls. The large extension to the original building tried to match the original and, for its time, was a good effort. In the early nineteenth century there came the English compromise in house style – the semi-detached. In it, two houses could be made to appear as one – even when those that could afford to live in them could clearly have afforded to live in detached houses. Later, of course, the ubiquitous terrace became the most popular type of house, and still is, though there is a huge architectural gulf between the elegant semis of the early and mid-Victorian period and the little boxes built today.

Industrial Buildings and Bridges

It is often a bit of surprise to those who think of Worcester as a picturesque cathedral city to realize that it is, and nearly always has been, an important industrial city as well – ever since Roman times. Today it is noted particularly for its engineering, but in the past was mainly renowned for its cloth trade, glove-making, and porcelain. Other trades have been identified through archaeological excavation, ranging from bone-working to bell-making as well as the normal service industries expected in any major medieval settlement. Of these there are few traces above ground, but Worcester has a surprisingly impressive, and varied, collection of mainly nineteenth-century industrial buildings – and the area around Lowesmore and Shrub Hill is particularly rich in these overlooked architectural treasures.

Much of Worcester's success as a city derives from it being a natural transport centre in the borderland between the western hills and the Midland plain. The site was also close to the tidal limit of the Severn and a rare bridging point with two natural fords. The old medieval bridge across the river may have been a direct successor to a possible Roman one, and may even have contained fragments of it. No one really knows, but it is thought that there was a stone bridge at

100 The much rebuilt Powick Bridge was the scene of the first engagement of the Civil War. Behind it is the former hydroelectric plant

Worcester by 1313. It was reached by Newport Street on the city side, and by the oddly named Turkey on the other bank, now Tybridge. In the early 1760s, by when it was no doubt much rebuilt, it was described as 'an antient, spacious, strong building consisting of six arches'. Despite this, in 1764 an Act was obtained to demolish it and build a new one farther downstream. The old bridge proved difficult to pull down, partly because Roman slag had been used in the piers. The architect chosen for the new bridge was John Gwynne, who built two other bridges across the river further upstream, at Shrewsbury and Atcham. The elegant Worcester bridge was opened in 1781, but the ever-increasing demands of motor traffic led to its being rebuilt in 1931. The city has now expanded its boundaries southwards to the River Teme, so the

101 Worcester has always been a transport centre, though little survives of its former importance as a road centre. This octagonal toll-house at Barbourne was built in the late eighteenth century when two separate turnpike trusts decided one joint venture was more efficient than two individual ones

old and new bridges at Powick are now partly within it. The old bridge of stone and brick is late medieval but has been rebuilt many times, the last major change after being deliberately broken in the Civil War. The cast-iron bridge nearby has Gothick detailing and was erected in 1837 as part of a general road improvement. It is not dissimilar to bridges designed by the great engineer Thomas Telford, but is credited to William Capper.

The Severn was a principal transport artery all the way from the Welsh hills near Welshpool, down through Shropshire, Worcestershire and Gloucestershire, and so to the sea. Indeed, in the eighteenth century it was by far the busiest river in Britain, and the second busiest in Europe. The river was an ancient right of way, the 'King's High Stream of Severn', and no tolls were charged for its use. This meant that little was done to maintain or improve the navigation. Only in the 1840s was the section upstream to Worcester finally altered, with the creation of weirs and locks, including one at Diglis, under the supervision of the engineer William Cubitt. It was too late, in many ways, because the new steam railways were about to attract the riverborne traffic. Schemes were made to improve

102 The 'new' Powick Bridge was built to the designs of William Capper in 1837 and has Tudor Gothic detailing in the side arches. The cast-iron main bridge still carries all the heavy traffic to and from the south-west after all these years

102 A detail of the Powick Bridge's Gothick parapet

103 The Worcester & Birmingham Canal opened in 1815. Originally planned to end at a basin in Lowesmore, it was extended instead to the river at Diglis. The 'bridge-with-the-hole-in-it' carried the Worcester–Hereford branch line, opened in 1860, over the canal at Lowesmore

104 The Hereford branch line crosses The Foregate by a single-span bridge that has become a feature of Worcester's townscape. It was remodelled in 1909

105 Inside Shrub Hill station is this lovely piece of 'railwayana' – a waiting room framed in cast-iron made locally by the Vulcan Iron Works and infilled with splendid glazed tiles from Maw's Ltd, of Jackfield, up the river in Shropshire

106 In 1864 the Worcester Engine Works was founded and the company set about the construction of a very ambitious works in Shrub Hill. Sadly the venture failed, leaving the legacy of one of the finest industrial façades in the country. This is the centre-piece, probably designed by Thomas Dickson

the river in the early 1900s, but it gradually decayed as trade fell off. Then, at the end of the 1920s, an oil storage depot served by barges was built at Diglis and the river traffic increased to such an extent that by 1938 it was greater than that being carried by rail. In 1944 a new wharf was built, capable of taking 280 ton barges and there were ambitious, but eminently sensible, plans to increase traffic after the war. Sadly it came to nothing, because of the spread of oil-pipelines and road tankers, and traffic petered out in the mid-1960s. The Diglis area is gradually being redeveloped, but the 1840s lock-keeper's house still stands.

The former Worcester & Birmingham Canal was opened throughout at the end of 1815 and did much to boost the industrial development of Lowesmoore. It is still in use, but remarkable devoid of interesting buildings. Even the Lowesmoore Basin, though an attractive place to watch the

narrowboats manoeuvring in the summer, is surrounded by that are all modern buildings.

Worcester now has two railways stations. Shrub Hill opened in 1850 but the station was rebuilt in 1865 by Edward Wilson. Despite its dark brick, this neo-Georgian façade flanked by drives sweeping up to its main entrance is a fine composition deliberately designed to look a little like a grand country mansion. Because of the ugly Elgar House in front of it, it is now only possible to see the full effect of the design from a three-quarter view. One little gem inside the station is a waiting room, formerly for ladies, built of delicate cast iron and completely encased in patterned glazed tiles from the Jackfield factory of Maw's Ltd, in the Ironbridge Gorge.

In 1860 a line was opened from Shrub Hill to Hereford, crossing the nearby canal on an unusual bridge. This has a single large span over the canal, a smaller archway over the tow-path, and, above that, a completely circular opening – a veritable bridge with a hole in it. This was presumably an attempt to take weight out of the structure without weakening it. On this branch, by The Foregate, is the city's second station,

109 On the South Quay, just downstream from the bridge, these converted Victorian hop and seed warehouses are a reminder of the former importance of the river trade to the city. Thankfully they have found new uses and have been sympathetically dealt with

110 The former mid-nineteenth-century Barbourne brewery has been converted into apartments. This is the view looking down Ashcroft Road. On the left is the former malting kiln, the malting floors being in the longer lower range to the right

111 For a while another way of producing alcoholic beverages was important in Worcester, there being a distillery on the west side of the river by the bridge. On the city side, in 1897, the company built the Rectifying House, where the spirits were refined. However, this portion of it, with its distinctive mock timber-framing, has been a public house or restaurant for most of this century

a fairly forgettable affair. The only interest here is the arched iron bridge over The Foregate itself, refaced in its present form in 1909 and very much part of the city's streetscape.

Connected with the railways is one of the largest and most impressive industrial façades of nineteenth-century England, occupying most of the east side of Shrub Hill Road. It was a product of the second 'Railway Mania' of the 1860s, begun in 1864 as the Worcester Engine Works and designed to build rolling stock – from locomotives to goods wagons – for the ever-expanding railway networks. The project, with an authorized capital of £300,000, was hugely ambitious – and failed miserably. Only eighty-four locomotives were built before the works closed in 1871. The buildings, probably designed by Thomas Dickson, amazingly survive, despite having been subdivided several times over the years and being changed internally. The central block contained the main fitting shops, the light fitting shops were to the left, and the pattern shops and foundry to the right. At the corner of Shrub Hill and Tolladine Road is the distinctive clock tower building and to the rear were a whole series of other workshops and sidings.

112 Already a piece of architectural history, this former garage and car showroom in Castle Street, originally called Austin House, was built in 1939 by J. Soutar

The distinctive red and yellow brick and the central pediment can be found in other industrial buildings in the town, such as the former Vinegar Works between St Martin's and Pheasant streets, with a virtually identical pedimented façade to each. This was built at around the same time as the Worcester Engine Works by Hill, Evans & Company, founded in 1830. The main part contained a huge filling hall, 160 ft long and 120 ft wide. The works continued to produce vinegar until 1966 and were subsequently converted into light industrial units.

The present façade of the Royal Worcester porcelain factory in Severn Street was also built in the mid-nineteenth century, although one building is of eighteenth-century date. Considering the tremendous and deserved fame of the products of this factory, its architecture is a little disappointing.

Worcester has one surprising industrial building, at Powick, the southern extremity of the expanded city. On the bank of the Teme is the first municipal hydroelectric power-station in England, and built at a total cost of over £21,000 by Thomas Rowbottom of Birmingham and opened in November 1894. The water-powered plant was backed up by steam power, hence the tall chimney that dominates the site. Surprisingly, the plant remained in use for well over half a century, finally closing in 1950. It is now occupied by industrial units and known, misleadingly, as Powick Mills.

Further Reading

Local Books

Dyer, A.D., *The City of Worcester in the Sixteenth Century* (1973)
Gwilliam, W., *Old Worcester: People and Places* (1993)
Hughes, P. (ed.), *Worcester Streets: Blackfriars* (1986)
Hughes, P. and Molyneux, N., *Worcester Streets: Friar Street* (1984)
Lane, J., *Worcester Infirmary in the Eighteenth Century* (1993)
Whitehead, D., *The Book of Worcester* (1976)

General Books

Brunskill, R.W., *Timber Building in Britain* (1985)
——, *Brick Building in Britain* (1990)
Clifton-Taylor, A., *The Pattern of English Building* (4th ed. 1987)
Cruickshank, D., & Burton, N., *Life in the Georgian City* (1990)
Harris, R., *Discovering Timber-Framed Buildings* (1978)
Pevsner, N., *The Buildings of England* series, in county volumes
Platt, C., *The English Medieval Town* (1976)

Index

Page numbers in bold indicate illustrations